Max
And his Big Imagination
Castles and knights
Activity Book

For Kids Ages 3-5

Max
And his Big Imagination

 **CASTLE KNIGHTS ACTIVITY BOOK**

by
Chrissy Metge

all about Me

All about:

This is me:

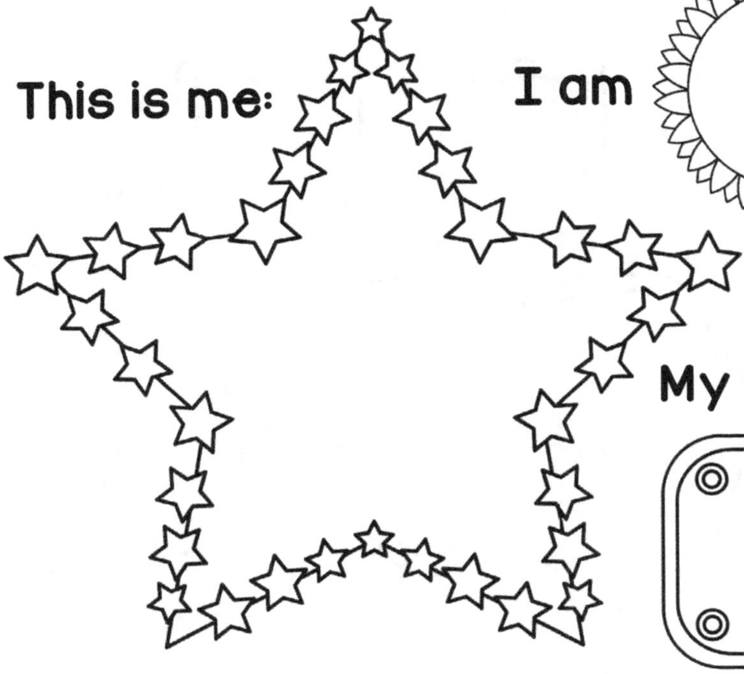

I am  ___ years old.

My favorite colour:

My birthday:

WARM UP WORK

Follow the lines.

⭐ DRAW IN THE SHAPES ⭐

Fill in the shapes with anything you want!

DRAW IN THE SHAPES

Fill in the shapes with anything you want!

FINISH THE PICTURE

Design your own knight!

HOW TO DRAW

Learn how to draw a castle!

HOW TO DRAW

Draw your castle here.

FIND THE PATH

Find the path to the horse.

FINISH THE PICTURE

Finish the castle drawing.

FIND AND COUNT

Make a trail from the knight to the castle following the numbers 1 to 20.

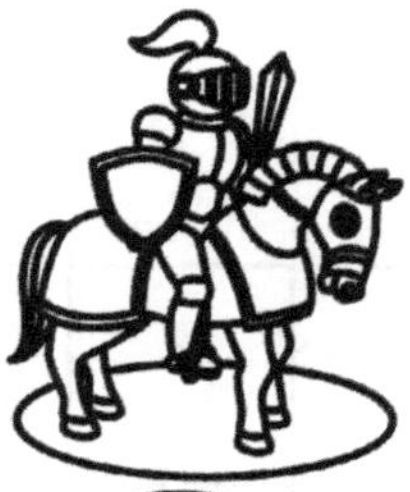

1	A	I	O	Y	D
2	3	4	5	F	J
C	8	7	6	N	P
10	9	K	15	16	17
11	12	13	14	R	18
E	M	U	H	L	19
G	Q	W	Z	B	20

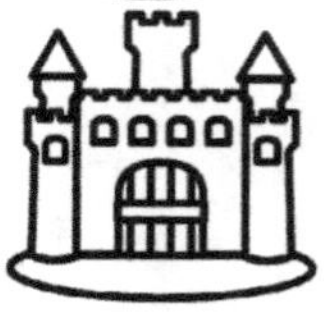

COLOUR THE PICTURE

Colour the knight!

HOW TO DRAW

Learn how to draw a horse!

HOW TO DRAW

Draw your horse here.

CONNECT THE DOTS

Connect the dots from A to Z.

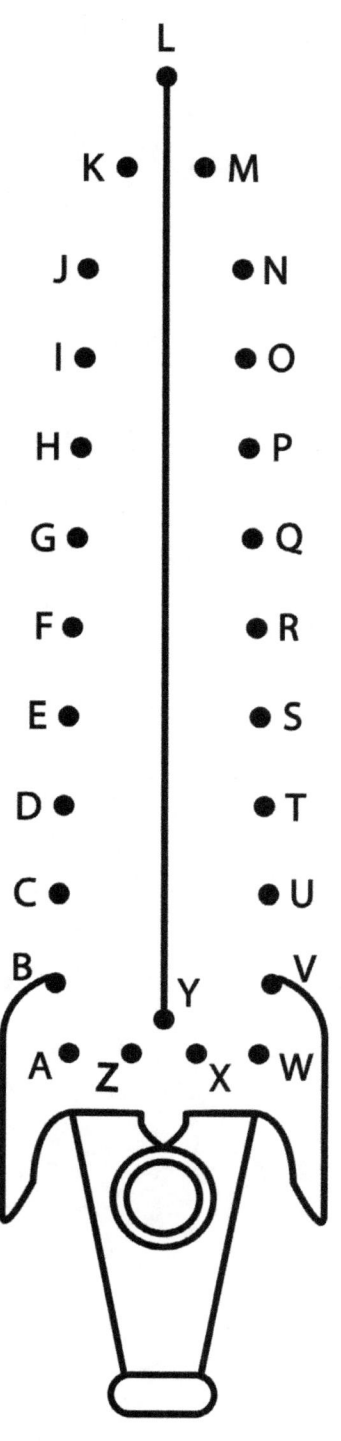

TRACE THE LETTERS

Colour the shields and trace the letters.

a b c d e
f g h i j
k l m n o
p q r s t
u v w
x y z

FINISH THE PICTURE

Finish the knight's horse.

FIND THE PATH

Find the path to the castle.

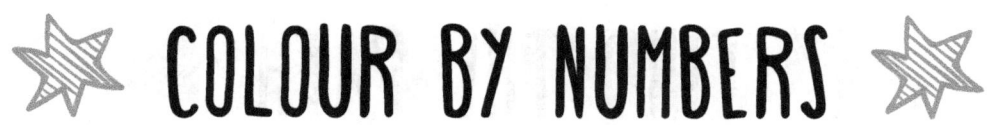

COLOUR BY NUMBERS

Use the colour key to colour the picture.

1 = red   3 = green   5 = brown
2 = blue   4 = yellow   6 = grey

MATCH THE PICTURE

Draw a line to the matching shadows.

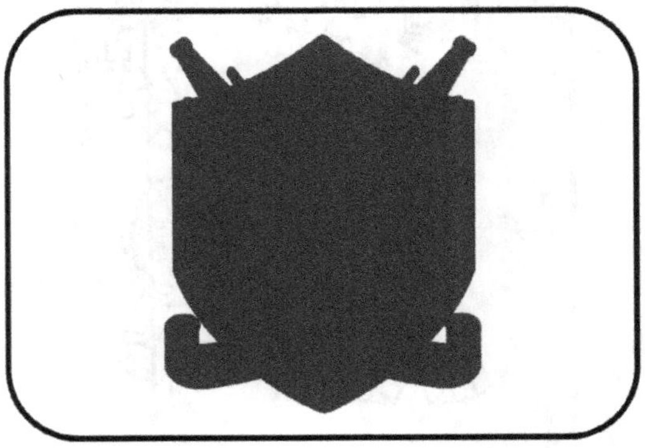

COUNT AND WRITE

Count the elements and write the numbers below.

FINISH THE DRAWING

Design your own castle!

SPOT THE DIFFERENCE

Find the differences between the two pictures.

FIND THE PATH

Help the knight find the dragon.

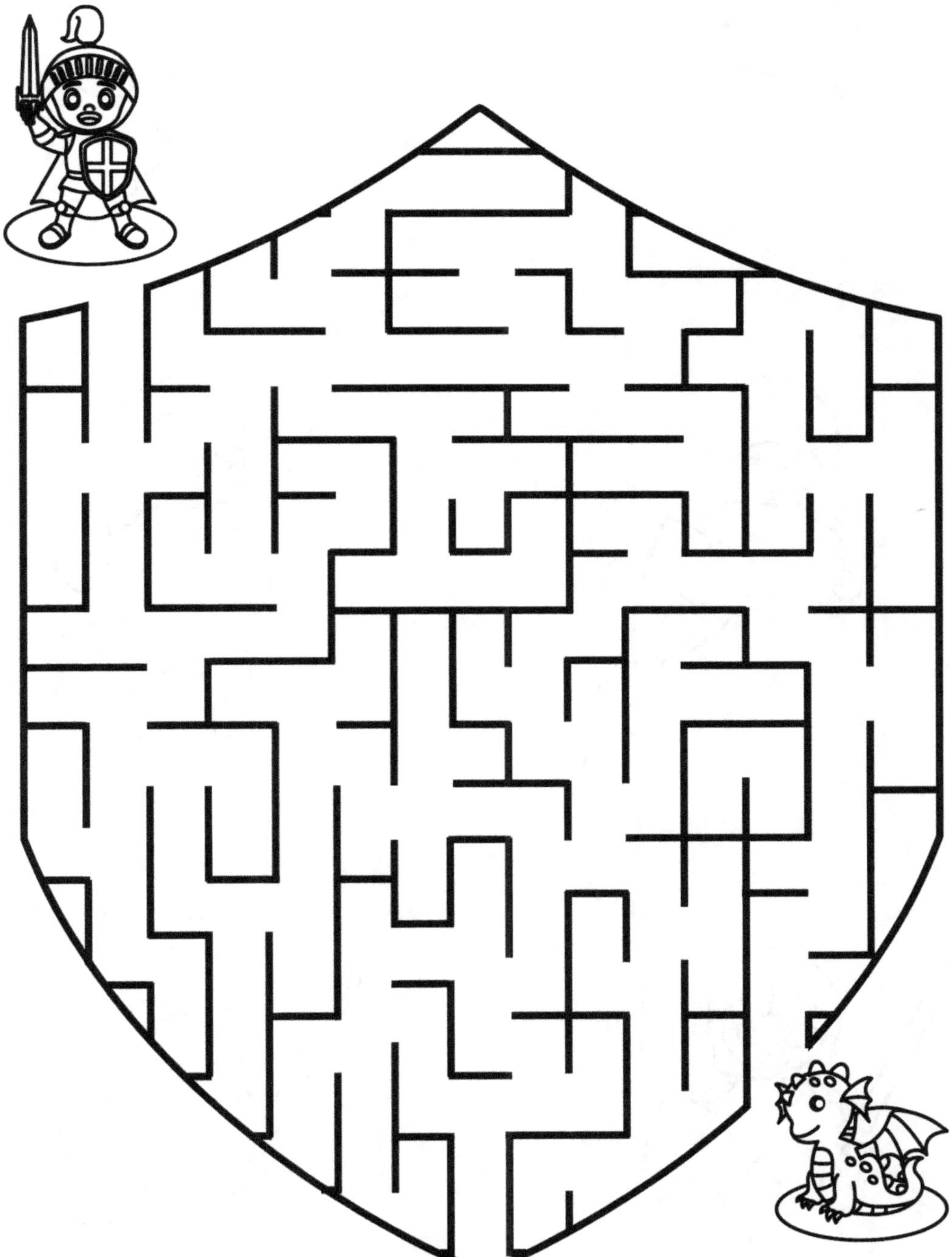

HOW TO DRAW

Learn how to draw a knight!

HOW TO DRAW

Draw your knight here.

CONNECT THE DOTS

Connect the dots from 1 to 20.

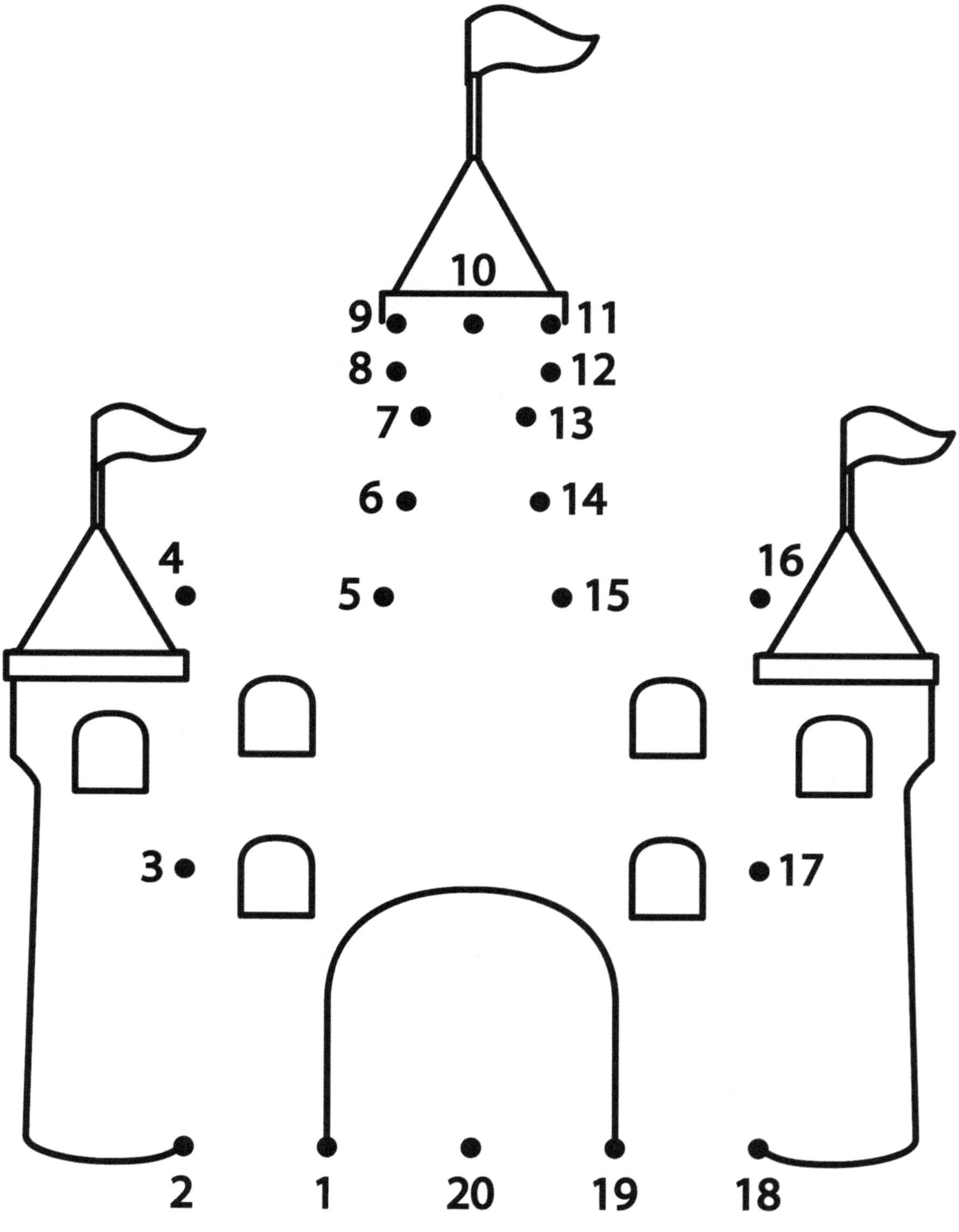

FINISH THE PICTURE

Design your own Coat of arms, cut out and hang on your wall.

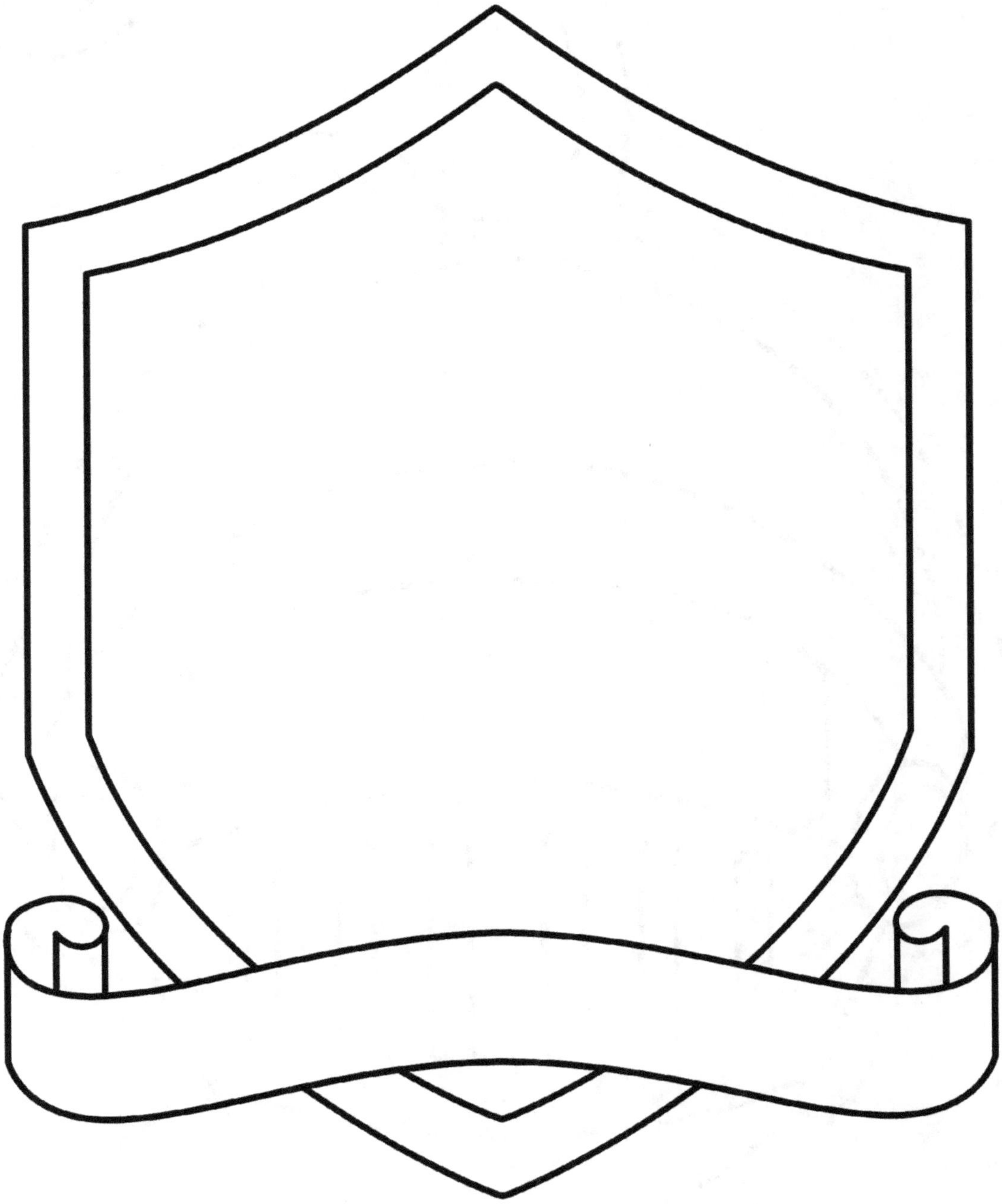

COLOUR AND CUT

Colour and cut out the mask.

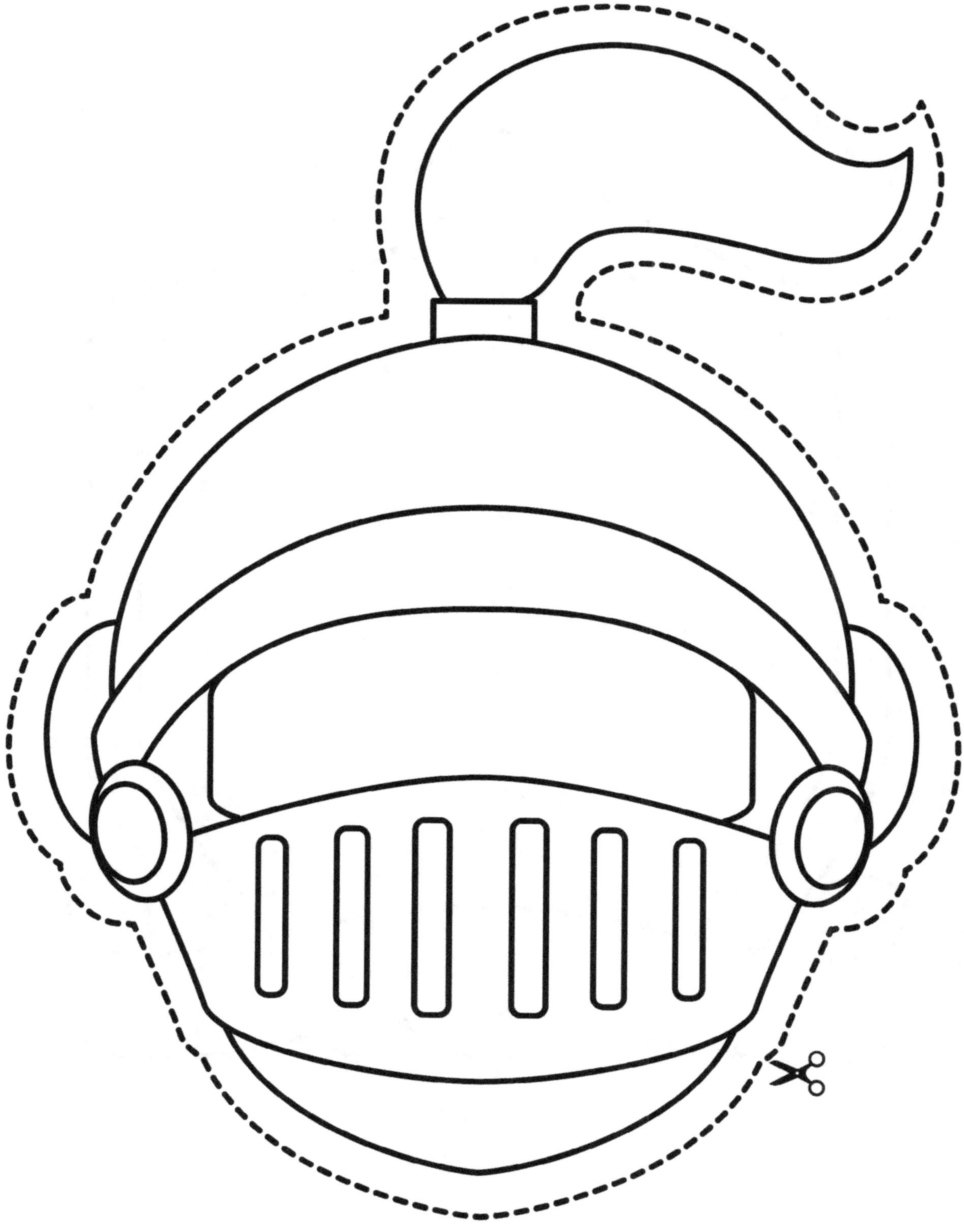

 # WHAT COMES NEXT?

Cut out and find the matching picture.

Max
And his Big Imagination

Check out our other activity books!

Transport Activity Book
Space Activity Book
Dinosaur Activity Book
Seaside Activity Book
Safari Activity Book

Read, Play, Imagine!

www.ducklingpublishing.com

Read, Play, Imagine!

Max is a little boy with a huge imagination, his adventures are to encourage and inspire children to use their imagination wherever they are!

Duckling publishing

www.chrissymetge.com
www.ducklingpublishing.com

www.ingramcontent.com/pod-product-compliance
Lightning Source LLC
Chambersburg PA
CBHW081436300426
44108CB00016BA/2385